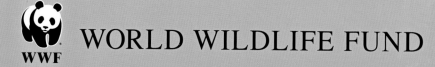

WORLD WILDLIFE FUND

Where Do

ISBN 0-7683-2044-5

Published in 1998 by Cedco Publishing Company,
100 Pelican Way, San Rafael, CA 94901.
Produced by Jennifer Barry Design, Sausalito, CA.

For a free catalog of our entire line of books, write us at the address above,
visit our website: www.cedco.com or e-mail us at: sales@cedco.com

Photography Credits
front cover: ©Tom & Pat Leeson
title page: ©Jeff Hunter, Image Bank
page 7: ©Tom & Pat Leeson
page 9: ©Kennan Ward
page 11: ©Jeff Hunter, Image Bank
page 13: ©Kevin Schafer
page 15: ©Gerry Ellis, ENP Images
page 17: ©Daniel J. Cox, Natural Exposures
page 19, cover flap: ©Tom Vezo; under flap: ©Larry Ulrich
page 21, cover flap: ©Art Wolfe; under flap: ©Kevin Schafer
page 23, cover flap: ©Dwight Kuhn; under flap: ©Lynn M. Stone
page 25, cover flap: ©Steve Gettle, ENP Images; under flap: ©Brian Kenney
page 27, cover flap: ©Joseph Drivas, Image Bank; under flap: ©Dwight Kuhn
page 29: ©Art Wolfe

Some photographs have been digitally-manipulated to produce this book.

I Live?

I am a Red Fox.

I hunt for rodents, birds,

and sometimes frogs.

I hide in dark,

safe places.

Where do I live?

I am a Polar Bear.

I have thick, white fur

that keeps me warm.

I play on the

snow and ice.

Where do I live?

I am an **Angelfish.**

I am brightly colored
and my body is very flat.

I can dart easily
into tight places.

Where do I live?

I am a Gorilla.

I eat leaves and

sometimes fruit.

I can walk on

two legs or four.

Where do I live?

I am a Zebra.

My black and white
stripes make it easy for
me to hide from lions.

I graze and live
in wide, open places.

Where do I live?

I am an Emperor Penguin.

I have three layers of

feathers to keep me warm.

I dive deep into

icy water to find

fish to eat.

Where do I live?

I am a **Pelican**.

I catch fish and store it
in a pouch in my beak.

I can fly, swim, and
dive in the water.

Where do I live?

I am a Camel.
I can go a long time
without drinking water.
I can carry heavy loads
on my back across
very hot sand.
Where do I live?

I am a Bullfrog.
I can swim and hold my breath underwater for a long time. My strong legs and webbed toes help me to be a good swimmer.
Where do I live?

I am an Egret.

I have beautiful,

white silky feathers.

I use my long bill to poke

for food in the mud.

Where do I live?

I am a Bee.

I buzz around flowers
and collect their pollen.

I take the pollen
to other flowers
to help them grow.

Where do I live?

I am a Sea Star.
I have five arms and
cling to rocks and coral.
I can be found in shallow
water close to the beach.
Where do I live?

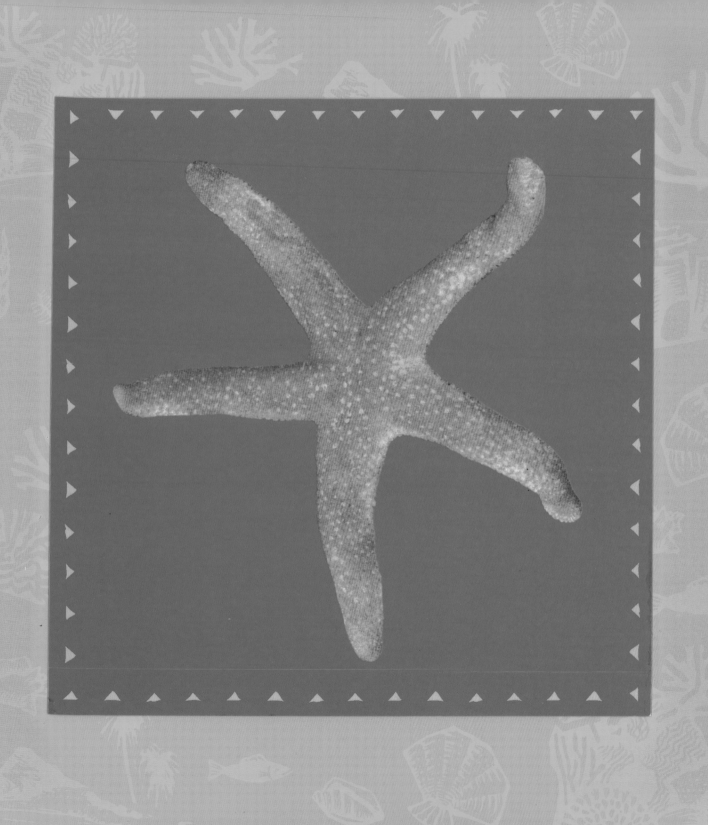

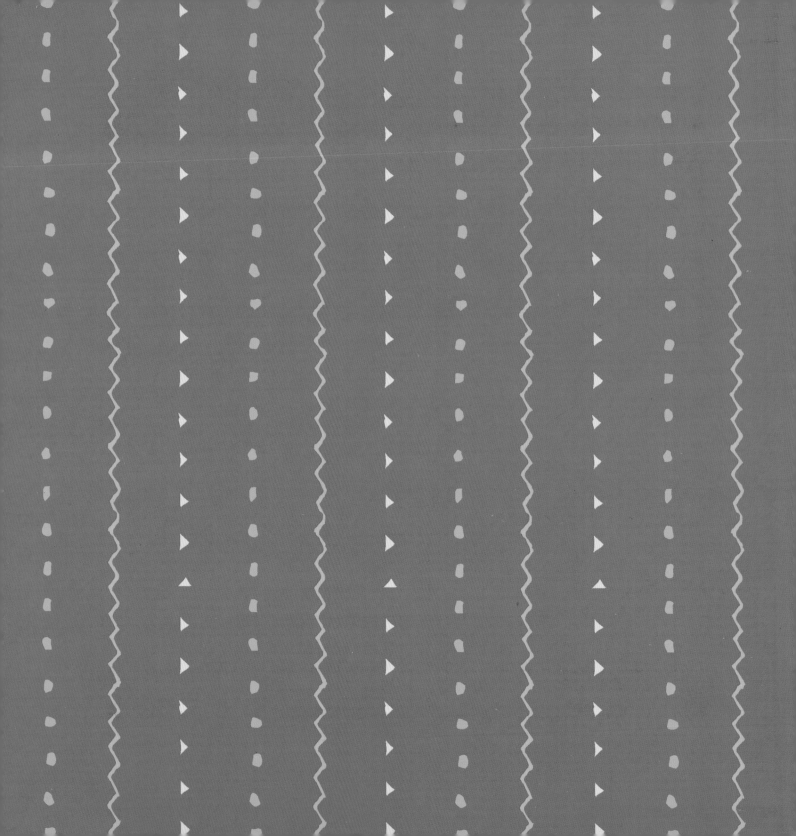